D1030081

Technology Timelines

MUSIC TECHNOLOGY

BROWN BEAR BOOKS

Published by Brown Bear Books Ltd

4877 N. Circulo Bujia
Tucson, AZ 85718
USA

and

First Floor
9-17 St. Albans Place
London N1 0NX

ISBN: 978-1-78121-240-0

Library of Congress Cataloging-in-Publication Data
available upon request

Author: Tom Jackson
Designer: Lynne Lennon
Picture Researcher: Clare Newman
Children's Publisher: Anne O'Daly
Design Manager: Keith Davis
Editorial Director: Lindsey Lowe

Manufactured in the United States of America

CPSIA compliance information: Batch# AG/5568

Picture Credits

The photographs in this book are used by permission
and through the courtesy of:

Key: b = bottom, c = center, l = left, r = right, t = top.

Front cover: tl, ©Dan Johansson; tr, ©Yury Shirokov/
Dreamstime; bl, ©Christopher King/Dreamstime;
br, © Lava Electronics.
Interior: 1, ©Sony; 4c, ©iStock/Thinkstock;
4-5b, ©Claudio Balducelli/Dreamstime; 5t, ©Ricjie81/
Shutterstock; 5br, ©Wikipedia; 6bl, ©Wikipedia;
6-7, ©James Steidl/Shutterstock; 7cr, ©Richie Lomba/
Dreamstime; 7bl, ©Terence Mendoza/Shutterstock;
7br, ©Wikipedia; 8b, ©Library of Congress;
8-9, ©Velora/Shutterstock; 9cr, ©Ronald Caswell/
Shutterstock; 9b, ©Wikipedia; 10b, ©Hakuna Jina/
Shutterstock; 10-11, ©Gelpi JM/Shutterstock;
11b, ©Wikipedia; 10b, ©Four Oaks/Shutterstock;
12-13t, ©Sizov/Shutterstock; 12-13b, ©iStock/
Thinkstock; 14b, ©Photo House/Shutterstock;
14-15, ©I Love Photo/Shutterstock; 15t, ©Wikipedia;
15bl, ©Hekandshoot/Shutterstock; 15br, ©Wikipedia;
16-17, ©Wikipedia; 17cr, ©Daniel Draghici/
Dreamstime; 17bl, ©iStock/Thinkstock; 17br, ©Anaken
2012/Shutterstock; 18b, ©ValeStock/Shutterstock;
18-19, ©Steve Collender/Shutterstock;
19, ©Wikipedia; 20bl, ©Alexander Sysoev/
Shutterstock; 20br, ©Ian Tragen/Shutterstock;
20-21, ©Sergej Razvodovskjj/Shutterstock;
21b, ©iStock/Thinkstock; 22, ©iStock/Thinkstock;
22-23, ©iStock/Thinkstock; 23cr, ©iStock/Thinkstock;
23br, ©Anada Panda/Shutterstock; 24br, ©iStock/
Thinkstock; 24-25, ©Sony; 25cr, ©Getty Images News/
Thinkstock; 25br, ©Getty Images Entertainment/
Thinkstock; 26 , ©SO47/Shutterstock; 26-27, ©Dedi
Grigoroiu/Shutterstock; 27tr, ©iStock Editorial/
Thinkstock; 27br, ©iStock/Thinkstock; 28, ©AFP/Getty;
29tr, ©Grant Hodhson/Splash News/Corbis;
29br, ©Digital Vision/Getty.

Brown Bear Books has made every attempt to contact
the copyright holder. If you have any information
please contact licensing@brownbearbooks.co.uk

All other photographs and artworks © Brown Bear Books Ltd.

Contents

Introduction

Sound is the main way people communicate. We use our voice to explain ideas, and songs are probably the oldest form of entertainment. Sounds are waves, or vibrations, in the air. Our ears pick up the vibrations and send signals to the brain, which we hear as sound. Until the 1800s, every sound was unique—once it was made, it could never be heard again. Recording technology changed all that.

Spreading News

Before music players were invented, songs were played by wandering musicians called minstrels. They traveled around the country performing the latest songs and reciting poetry. As well as providing entertainment, minstrels also spread important news as they moved from town to town.

Amphitheater

In ancient times, the best place to hear music was in amphitheaters. These were built on the side of a curved hill. The audience sat in a semicircle (sometimes a full circle) around the stage. Sound bounced around the amphitheater, so that all could hear it clearly.

Playing Loud

The alpine horn is used in the mountainous regions of Switzerland. The large size makes the horn very loud, so it can be heard across the mountains. A similar shape of horn was used in early music players to make sounds louder.

« A DIFFERENT VIEW »

AN UNDERWATER CONCERT

In 1855, the tsar of Russia, Alexander II, held a party around Kronstadt harbor, and an unusual music system was designed to fill the area with sound. A trio of musicians was lowered into the water inside a submarine. Sound travels very well through water, so when the band played, its music was heard rising up out of the water!

Phonograph

The first sound recorder was invented in **1877**. It worked by converting the vibrations of a sound wave in air into a solid form. Playing the solid recording would recreate the original sound.

An American inventor, Thomas Edison, invented a machine called the phonograph. The name means "voice writer." It was designed to record speech but worked with music, too.

THE HORN *was used to capture the voice for recording and for playing back the sound.*

Phonograph

To record on this device, you spoke into the horn, while winding a cylinder. The sound wave made a needle vibrate while it cut a groove into a sheet of tinfoil on the cylinder. Running the needle back through the same groove made it vibrate the air, which came out of the horn as sound!

A VIBRATING PLATE *was attached to the needle, which scratched a groove on the cylinder.*

TIMELINE

1857

Phonautograph

Édouard-Léon Scott de Martinville invents a device for turning sound vibrations into a wavy pattern on glass (right). The sound could not be played back.

1880s

Wax Cylinders

The original foil cylinders used in the phonograph are replaced by ones made from soft wax (right).

A SHEET OF TINFOIL covered the cylinder. Later versions use wax instead of foil.

THE CYLINDER, or mandrel, was turned during recording and to play back the sound.

THOMAS EDISON

Thomas Edison was also involved in creating many other types of modern technology. They include the film camera, the light bulb, and microphones. He was also one of the first people to build power plants and set up an electrical power network.

A HANDLE was used to turn the cylinder during recording and playback.

1895

Shellac Discs

Wax cylinders were very fragile. Shellac, a plasticlike resin made by insects, was used to make more permanent records.

Gramophone

The gramophone played music using a similar system to the phonograph, only it used flat record discs instead of cylinders.

The gramophone, or record player, was invented in 1887 by German Emile Berliner. It was entirely mechanical, just like Edison's machine. The big advantage was that the records, made from hard shellac, were easier to duplicate in large numbers. That created a recording industry, where people could buy records of music from all over the world.

Mechanical Gramophone

The gramophone was not capable of making its own recordings but could play records produced in a number of sizes. The turntable was powered by a clockwork motor. When the motor began to run out of power, the music would slow down.

A RECORD DISC made of shellac sits on a turntable.

TIMELINE

1902

Recording Artist
An Italian singer, Enrico Caruso, becomes the first world-famous recording artist.

1920

Radio Entertainment
The first regular radio programs are broadcast in the U.S. In the UK a transmitter (right) begins playing British Broadcasting Corporation (BBC) programs.

A LARGE HORN amplified the sound coming from the needle, so it was loud enough to hear.

THE NEEDLE'S vibrations wobble a metal disc, creating sound waves.

PIANOLA

A pianola is a mechanical piano that plays complicated music recorded as a pattern of holes on a roll of thin card. Each note was indicated by a hole on the card and was played as it ran through a reader. Pianolas became most common in the 1920s. Some models were powered by a foot pump, while others had a small electric motor.

A HANDLE was used to wind up a clockwork mechanism. The clockwork slowly unwound and spun the turntable for several minutes.

1924

78 RPM

A standard speed for a gramophone record is agreed. The disc turned at 78 rotations per minute (RPM).

1925

Electric Playback

Magnetic pickups are introduced. They turn the vibrations of a gramophone needle into an electric signal, which is turned into sound.

Radio Set

By the 1930s, ordinary families could afford their own radio set. This device picked up music broadcast as radio waves. A receiver in the set would convert the radio waves into sound.

Radio waves are a form of radiation similar to light and heat. Electric wires can be made to glow and give out heat—and they can also transmit invisible radio waves. In 1897, Italian Guglielmo Marconi invented a radio transmitter that could give out radio waves that carried a signal.

Valve Radio

A receiver in the radio converted the signal into a tiny electric current. This current was boosted, or amplified, using valves, which were glass tubes a little like light bulbs. The current was now powerful enough to make the loudspeaker produce sound.

THE VOLUME KNOB controlled the amount of electric current at the loudspeaker. More current made the sound louder.

TIMELINE

1931
Stereophonic
The idea of stereo is introduced, where two different sounds are recorded at the same time. The technology took several more years to develop.

1933
Electric Guitar
A guitar is designed that uses magnetic pickups to detect the vibrations of its strings.

1939
Magnetophon
The first tape recorder is designed. It records sound as a pattern of magnetic iron grains on a plastic tape.

THE CASE was made of wood. The radio was a large object and often had its own stand or cabinet.

THE LOUDSPEAKER was hidden behind a cloth covering.

THE RADIO FREQUENCY is shown on the front to make tuning easier.

THE POWER switch needed to be turned on well before the program started, so that the valves had a chance to warm up to the right temperature.

TUNING was controlled by turning a knob.

« A DIFFERENT VIEW »

SOUNDTRACKS

Early movies (or "moving pictures") had no sound, The first "talkie" (a movie with talking) was shown in 1927. A soundtrack ran alongside the pictures on the film. The light that projected the pictures also shone through the soundtrack. That made a flickering beam that was converted into sound by a light-sensitive detector.

Pictures

Stereo soundtrack

D65 X C9V 89

1945

Wire Recorder

Simpler than tape technology, wire recorders become common. Sound is recorded as magnetized and demagnetized sections on a moving wire.

1948

Singles and LPs

New record formats are introduced. The 45 RPM "single" stores a three-minute song on each side. The larger Long Player (LP) is played at 33.3 RPM and stores 40 minutes of music.

Record Player

In the 1950s, the radio set became part of a music "console," which also included a record player. This was an electrical gramophone that used an amplifier to produce sound.

THE RECORD had grooves on both sides. A scratch in the groove would make the needle jump or get stuck.

The record player was still the best music player there was, even 70 years after it had been invented. But there had been many improvements. An electric motor drove the turntable, while the vibrations of the needle were converted into a small electric current that was then amplified as in a radio set.

THE TURNTABLE was turned by an electric motor and had three set speeds—78, 45, and 33.3 RPM.

Vinyl Record Player

By the 1950s, all records were made from a plastic called vinyl. The recorded groove was pressed into a disc when it was warm and soft. A vinyl record had a narrower groove than older styles, so more music could fit on each side.

A VENT lets out the heat produced by the vacuum tubes, or valves, that were used as amplifiers.

TIMELINE

1950

Jukebox
Jukeboxes playing 45 RPM "singles" become common in the United States. The coin-operated jukebox plays a selected song on request.

1951

The Top 40
A chart of popular songs is started in the United States. Number 1 in the chart is the song that is the most popular that week.

A MAGNETIC CARTRIDGE converted the vibrations of the needle into a fluctuating electric current.

THE LOUDSPEAKER was hidden inside.

A RADIO was included in the wooden console.

BUTTONS were used to tune the radio to preset radio stations.

RECORD PLAYERS

Sound is recreated by a needle vibrating as it runs through a long groove. The groove runs all around the surface of the record. The needle is connected to a magnet, and its motion creates a tiny fluctuating electric current. That current is amplified to make it strong enough to power loudspeakers. These then turn the electric current into sounds we can hear.

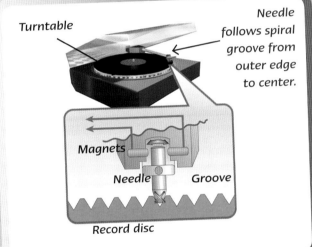

Turntable

Needle follows spiral groove from outer edge to center.

Magnets

Needle   Groove

Record disc

1954
Jack Plugs
Small plugs, known as jacks, are developed for connecting headphones to new portable radios and music players.

1956
Car Radio
Radio receivers that fit into the dashboard of a car are introduced, so that motorists can listen as they drive.

1962
Electret Microphone
A microphone uses an electrified magnet (electret) to convert vibrations into an electric signal. They are very small and still used today in telephones and computers.

Portable Radio

In 1954, the first transistor radios were introduced. Transistors are electronic devices that have made it possible to make music players much smaller.

A transistor is made from silicon and other semiconductor materials. Semiconductors can switch from being insulators that block electricity to conductors, which let it flow through. This aspect made transistors good amplifiers for boosting musical signals—and they were much smaller than old-fashioned valves.

Standard Radio

This transistor radio was made in Japan in 1962. Its case was made of plastic, and the small electronic components weighed 2.2 pounds (1 kg), so it was easy enough to carry around.

A HANDLE on top was used to carry the radio around.

THE LOUDSPEAKER was small but powerful enough to be heard when played outdoors.

POWER was provided by batteries at the turn of a knob.

TIMELINE

1963

Compact Cassette

A new tape system is introduced that stores a strip of magnetic tape on two reels inside a plastic cassette.

1964

Mobile Player

A battery-powered record player that can be carried in a suitcase is one of the first portable music players.

TRANSISTORS and other electronics replaced the large valves of earlier music players.

THE AERIAL was telescopic. It had to be fully extended to pick up radio signals.

« INSIDE OUT »

MICROPHONE AND SPEAKER

A microphone converts sound into an electrical signal. A loudspeaker turns that signal back into sound. Sound is a vibration, and that makes a magnet vibrate in the microphone. As the magnet moves, it creates a current in a detector. The intensity of this current rises and falls to match the sound's vibrations. In a speaker, the electric signal runs through a wire around a magnet, which is attached to a cone. The current makes the magnet and cone wobble, which pushes the air to make sound waves.

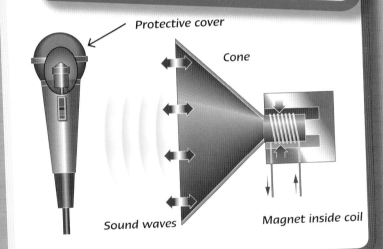

Protective cover

Cone

Sound waves

Magnet inside coil

1965

8-track Cartridge

A tape cartridge is invented. Eight-tracks are popular for use in car music systems (right).

1967

Quadrophonics

A system is developed for sending up to four different sound signals to different loudspeakers. It is used initially for live music concerts.

Hi-Fi

AN AMP, or amplifier, received inputs from the radio and turntable, then boosted them into a loud but clear sound.

As music players became more common, people wanted devices that created sounds that were as close as possible to the original live music. The hi-fi was the result.

The term *hi-fi* is short for "high fidelity," which is another way of saying "very faithful." So a hi-fi became the name for a music player that could play back recordings so they sounded as if the musicians were in the room, performing live.

Stereo Radio-Phonograph

This Italian hi-fi music center was the best money could buy in 1966. It played in stereo, so different instruments and voices could be heard coming from the left or right speakers. It also used the latest electronic amps, or amplifiers, which boosted the sound without adding unwanted noises.

KNOB CONTROLLERS were used to adjust the sound, changing the level of the deep bass and higher treble sounds. The volume in each speaker could also be adjusted.

TIMELINE

1970s

Cassette Recorders
Home recording systems become common using compact cassette recorders.

1971

Surround Sound
A quadrophonic system is developed for the home. Surround sound is designed to fill a room with music.

1974

Synthesizer
Music that uses artificial sounds created by electronic instruments called synthesizers (right) becomes popular.

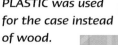

A LID prevented dust from getting on the turntable.

PLASTIC was used for the case instead of wood.

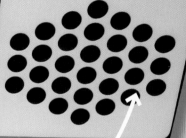

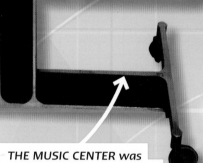

THE SPEAKERS were on either side of the music center to produce a stereo effect—with different sounds coming from each side.

THE MUSIC CENTER was an item of furniture and could be moved around the room.

« POWER PEOPLE »

RAY DOLBY

In 1966, this American engineer invented a way of reducing the hiss on music recordings, which is still used today. The Dolby system boosts the deep sounds during recording, so that they drown out any high-pitched hiss. During playback, deep sounds are turned down again to the correct level.

DOLBY

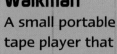

1979

Walkman

A small portable tape player that plays music into headphones is introduced by the Japanese company Sony.

Tape Deck

In the 1980s, compact cassette decks began to replace record players. The sound they made was not always better, but cassette tapes were much tougher that vinyl, and tape players were cheaper and easier to carry around.

A TWEETER, or small speaker, played the high-pitched sounds.

A WOOFER, or large speaker, played the lower-pitched sounds.

While transistor radios made it possible to listen to music outdoors or wherever you were away from home, you could not choose which songs were playing—and the radio's speakers were not very loud. That all changed with the 1980s boom box.

Boom Box

This double cassette deck could work anywhere, although it was a little too heavy to carry far. However, it could certainly play loud and so was ideal for use in halls, in parks, and at the beach.

TIMELINE

1981
Music TV
Pop stars produce videos of themselves performing songs. These are played on music TV channels, such as MTV.

1982
Compact Disc
A new format for music is launched, where music is stored on compact discs that are read by a laser beam.

1983
MIDI
The Musical Instrument Digital Interface (MIDI) allows musical instruments of all kinds to be connected to each other by computer.

18

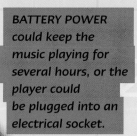

« INSIDE OUT »

TAPE RECORDING

Audio tape is coated in magnetic grains. An electrical signal from a microphone is converted into a magnetic field by the tape head. This field arranges the grains into a pattern. The head can also detect this magnetic pattern to play back the sounds.

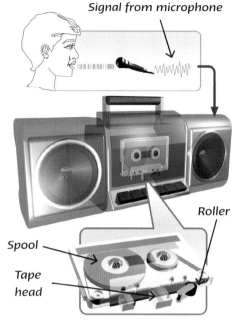

Signal from microphone

Roller

Spool

Tape head

No recording

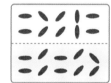

Recording

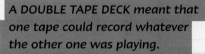

A DOUBLE TAPE DECK meant that one tape could record whatever the other one was playing.

1984

Discman

A portable compact disc player is launched, although it suffers from playback problems created by the disc wobbling around inside.

1987

Sampler

A drum machine that can play back "samples," or recorded sounds, in any rhythm is introduced.

Compact Disc

Music met computing in the 1990s, as compact disc players replaced tapes and records. The music on a CD is organized in the same way as a computer file.

Music played back from a tape or record contained a lot of extra sounds, such as echoes and hisses that were picked up during the recording. None of this unwanted sound was included on the CD, so a CD player could play music louder and clearer than ever before.

CD Player

The CD player was complicated because the 4.7-inch (12-cm) compact disc had to be spun faster when the laser was scanning near the middle and slowed down as it read around the edge. This was all controlled by a microprocessor similar to the ones used in computers.

A SCREEN displays information about the song being played, such as how long it has left to play.

TIMELINE

1988
Sport Walkman
A tough, waterproof version of the portable tape player is introduced for use during sports.

1993
MiniDisc
A new recording format is introduced (left). It uses the heat from a laser to create a magnetic record on a small 2.4-inch (6-cm) disc.

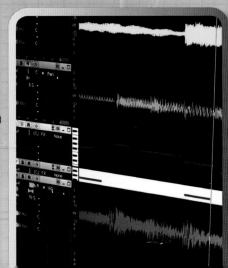

A LID must be closed for the music to play. It keeps the compact disc stable, so it does not wobble as it spins.

THE LOUDSPEAKERS can be placed anywhere in the room.

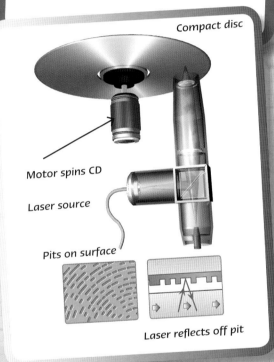

COMPACT DISC

A CD stores music as a pattern of pits, tiny hollows on its bottom surface. A laser is used to detect these dents by the way they reflect the light. The laser reads from the center and moves to the edge.

Compact disc

Motor spins CD

Laser source

Pits on surface

Laser reflects off pit

THE COMPACT DISC is made of plastic with a layer of aluminum inside that holds the pits.

1993

Digital Workstation
Software (left) that turns an ordinary computer into a mixing desk makes it possible to make music at home.

1995

Digital Radio
Digital radio (below) services are launched in Norway.

1996

Skip Protection
A memory chip added to a portable CD player stores 30 seconds of music before beginning to play. This keeps the player from losing its place and skipping songs when it is knocked or shaken.

Going Digital

By the twenty-first century, recordings of music and other types of audio could be stored as computer files, such as MP3s.

The MP3 file format was invented in 1996. It was a system for compressing the information in a sound recording. MP3s do this by only recording the parts of the music that the human ear can detect. Many quieter sounds played in the original performance are drowned out by louder ones. Even if a music player were to play them back, our ears could not hear them. An MP3 does not store them at all, and we cannot tell the difference. A CD stores 11 times as much information as an MP3 file, but the quality of the music is more or less the same. Being able to store music in this compressed form meant that MP3 players became pocket-sized gadgets.

A SCREEN displays information about songs. The device can also play videos and games and show photos.

PHOTOS 📷

THE EARPHONES are small enough to fit inside the ear. Other speakers could be plugged in, but they required their own battery power to play the music from this small MP3 player.

TIMELINE

1999

MP3 Player
The first MP3 player is released, playing music stored as computer files.

2002

Personal Radio
Last.fm, an Internet music service, begins. The service is a personal radio that plays songs matched to your preferences.

myspac
a plac

A JACK PLUG is the only output. It connects to headphones, a hi-fi, or small speakers.

EOS

MES

ICONS on the screen are used to control the player.

A HARD DISK inside stores the music and other files.

THE CONTROLS are used to select songs from lists shown on the screen.

« INSIDE OUT »

DIGITAL MUSIC

The term *digital* means "made of numbers." A sound wave in the air is changing continuously, but to be converted into digital form, the wave must be chopped up into millions of tiny sections that have a fixed size (or number). Each section represents an unchanging tone, but when they are played one after the other, we hear them as a rising and falling melody like the original live sound.

2003

Sharing Music
Myspace (left) starts up as an early social networking service. Recording artists use it as a place to promote their music to the public.

.com™
or friends

2005

Miniaturization
A tiny MP3 player, the iPod Shuffle, is introduced. It stores 240 songs on a microchip.

Music Apps

Because music could be made and stored as computer files, playing music became something that a computer did. The music player became one of the applications of a computer.

The first computers were designed to do complicated mathematics and remember large amounts of information. They still do those things, but the information they store also includes music files, and the complex math is put to work converting those files into our favorite songs.

THIS PLAYER has an amp and loudspeaker designed to work with a smartphone.

Smartphones

In 2007, the first smartphones were introduced. They were pocket-sized computers that ran small programs, or apps—short for "applications." The music app made the phone work just like a portable MP3 player.

AN ALARM CLOCK can be set to play music at a certain time.

TIMELINE

2006

Spotify
A music streaming service is introduced in Europe. It plays music and commercials like a radio station, but it allows members to choose the music they listen to.

2008

Wireless Headphones
Headphones that connect to a music player by a wireless Bluetooth connection become common.

CONTROLS on the dock take over from the phone when it is plugged in.

A SMARTPHONE includes a music player app that makes it work as an MP3 player.

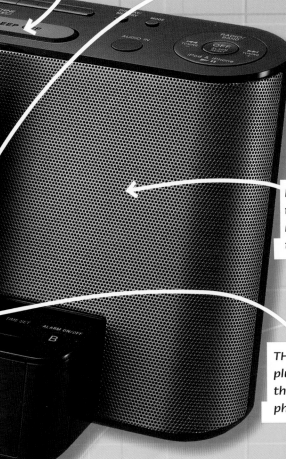

LOUDSPEAKERS in the panel play the music stored on the smartphone.

THE DOCK has a plug that connects the player to the phone.

STEVE JOBS

Steve Jobs, the cofounder of Apple computers, was the driving force behind iTunes, an online music store that was launched in 2001. iTunes allowed people to download songs and other audio files. These files were stored on a computer or transferred to an MP3 player.

2009

Audio Fingerprint

Apps are released that can recognize any song—whether played from a speaker, played on an instrument, or sung, hummed, or whistled.

2012

Music Video

The music video for South Korean pop star Psy's song "Gangnam Style" is the first video to be viewed a billion times on YouTube.

25

Modern Sounds

Today, music is played, stored, and created on computers. There are apps that help you write your own songs and record your own radio shows, and then share them among your friends.

Today's music players can be connected to the Internet. This allows you to buy the latest tracks as MP3 files and store them on your device. However, that is not the only way to listen to music. It is possible to stream songs through the Internet to your player, such as a smartphone or tablet. A file is not being downloaded. All that is being sent is the information needed for the headphones or speaker to make sound.

A WiFi CONNECTION allows music to be streamed from any computer on a home network or from the Internet.

MUSIC VIDEOS as well as songs can be downloaded and played on the tablet.

Spoken Word
Podcasts are audio programs that are not broadcast via a radio signal but are downloaded as MP3 files. You can listen to a show whenever you want and catch up with the ones you have missed. Podcasts became common in 2005.

PODCAST

THE LOUDSPEAKER is behind the screen.

Digital Instruments

A tablet computer, or another touchscreen device, can be converted into any musical instrument. The screen could become a piano keyboard, a drum machine, or a guitar with strings that play when swiped.

ICONS represent each group of songs. They can be arranged by artist, by album, or by name.

« A DIFFERENT VIEW »

ANECHOIC CHAMBER

To make digital music sound more like natural sounds, scientists need to understand how sound behaves. To do that, they use a studio called an anechoic chamber. The shaped walls of the chamber absorb all echoes, so that only one sound wave is being heard at a time.

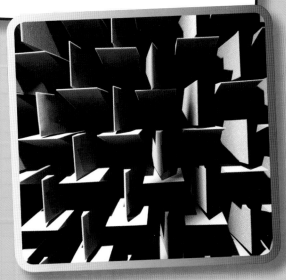

The Future of Music

Music is always changing, as new ideas and instruments are developed. It is impossible to guess at how music in the future will sound. Technology could make us all into musicians, or it could let us hear new music the moment it is created by our favorite artists.

Internet music services already allow us to hear music composed by millions of different artists. In the future, we might listen to music written by computers and performed by robots, or we might use technology to beam live concerts into our homes—making it feel like we are actually there.

SOUND

Robot Music

The members of this rock band are all robots. They can play the same instruments as human musicians and can be programmed to perform any song. However, they are also able to make up melodies. They are programmed with the same musical rules that human musicians use to improvise—or jam— new music.

Sharing Music

Today, music from all around the world is accessible on the Internet. Online sharing services, such as SoundCloud, means users can upload, record and share their music with other users. Founded in 2007, SoundCloud is used by 200 million people today.

Holograms

Live performances are a very exciting way of listening to music. Hologram technology, which projects a live moving image of a performer onto a stage, will make it possible for the world's most popular stars to appear in shows all over the world—all at the same time!

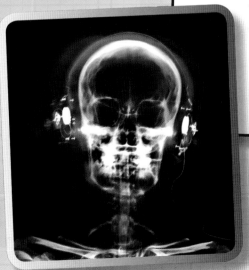

« A DIFFERENT VIEW »

VIBRATING BONE

The latest headphones do not send waves into the ears but into the bones of the jaw and skull. The vibration in the bones is picked up by ears, but the sound is too quiet for anyone else nearby to hear.

Glossary

aerial A wire or other long metal object used by a radio receiver to pick up a radio signal.

amplified To make louder or more powerful.

applications A program that makes a computer do a particular job. Examples of applications include: word processor, Web browser, and music player. Small applications are apps.

audio Another word for sound, most often referring to recorded sound.

Bluetooth A radio communication system where devices can connect to each other over short distances.

compress To reduce in size and make as small as possible.

digital Organized as a series of numbers, or digits. Computer files are always digital and are made up of long sequences of 1s and 0s.

disc A record or compact disc.

fidelity Another word for "faithfulness." In terms of music, *fidelity* refers to how close the playback is to the original sound.

fluctuating Rising and falling in a continuous but irregular way.

hard disk A computer memory system that stores files as magnetized patterns. Hard disks are used in large computers, video recorders, and early MP3 players.

hologram A 3-D image that can be viewed from all angles—just like a real object.

portable Small enough to carry.

software Another name for computer programs. A computing device itself is called the hardware, but it cannot work without software telling it what to do.

synthesizer A musical instrument that creates artificial sounds using electronics. The sounds may be copies of traditional instruments, or they may be completely new.

volume A measure of how loud a sound is.

WiFi A computer network that connects devices by a high-speed radio connection.

Further Resources

Books

Parker, Steve. *Tabletop Scientist: The Science of Sound: Projects and Experiments with Music and Sound Waves*. Mineola, NY: Dover Publications, 2013.

Spilsbury, Louise, and Richard Spilsbury. *The Radio* (Tales of Invention). Chicago: Heinemann-Raintree Library, 2011.

Throp, Claire. *Digital Music: A Revolution in Music*. Chicago: Heinemann-Raintree Library, 2011.

VanHecke, Susan. *Raggin' Jazzin' Rockin': A History of American Musical Instrument Makers*. Honesdale, PA: Boyds Mills Press, 2011.

Websites

artsedge.kennedy-center.org/ multimedia/series/AudioStories/ music-of-sound.aspx
Learn how music and sound work together in sound design.

electronics.howstuffworks.com/ home-audio-channel.htm
Find out how different music technologies work in this series of articles.

www.bgfl.org/bgfl/custom/ resources_ftp/client_ftp/ks2/ music/piano/
Turn your screen into a piano keyboard, and play melodies using different sounds.

www.hoffmanacademy.com
Learn how to play piano with this series of free video piano lessons from the Hoffman Academy.

www.nps.gov/edis/ photosmultimedia/very-early- recorded-sound.htm
Listen to some very early sound recordings, including some made by Thomas Edison himself.

www.sfskids.org/compose
Learn all about orchestral instruments and the elements that make up music at the San Francisco Symphony site.

Index